My Love Affair with
MIAMI BEACH

PHOTOGRAPHS
Richard Nagler

INTRODUCTION & COMMENTARY
Isaac Bashevis Singer

SIMON & SCHUSTER

New York   London   Toronto   Sydney   Tokyo   Singapore

SIMON AND SCHUSTER
Simon & Schuster Building
Rockefeller Center
1230 Avenue of the Americas
New York, New York 10020

1   3   5   7   9   10   8   6   4   2

Library of Congress Cataloging-in-Publication Data

Nagler, Richard.
    My love affair with Miami Beach / photographs by Richard Nagler
introduction and commentary by Isaac Bashevis Singer.
        p.   cm.
    ISBN: 0-671-74184-5
        1. South Beach (Miami Beach, Fla.)—Description—Views.   2. South
Beach (Miami Beach, Fla.)—Social   life and customs—Pictorial works.
3. Jews—Florida—Miami Beach—Pictorial works.   4. Miami Beach
(Fla.)—Description—Views.   5. Miami Beach (Fla.)—Social life and
customs—Pictorial works.   6. Singer, Isaac Bashevis, 1904–
—Homes and haunts—Florida—Miami Beach.   I. Singer, Isaac
Bashevis, 1904–   . II. Title.
F319.M62N24   1991
975.9′38—dc20   91-8762
                                                                                CIP

ISBN: 0-671-74184-5

Book Design by David Charlsen

Printed in Singapore

This book was inspired by and is lovingly dedicated to

Morris and Kate Sosnow
Sheila Sosnow and Ethan Sosnow Nagler
Sid and Madeleine Nagler

(Previous Page)
Park Scene, 6th and Ocean Drive   *November 1988*

My Love Affair with

MIAMI BEACH

by Isaac Bashevis Singer

When I first came to this country in 1935, I found that the winters in New York were terribly cold, like the winters in Poland. The winter of 1948 was particularly cold. People used to say it's warm in Miami Beach in the winter, but I couldn't believe it. I just could not believe that this is possible, that there is a place where it is warm in winter. I also heard about Miami Beach all kinds of stories that the place is vulgar, that the people are funny there. They said all kinds of things about Miami Beach, but if people are vulgar or crazy, I like to know about it.

My wife, Alma, and I had not had a vacation since we were married in 1940. We had been particularly poor in my early days as a writer in New York, but somehow we had managed to save a few dollars that cold winter in 1948, and we decided to buy two train tickets to Miami.

We traveled for a whole day and a night in the coach, sitting straight up in our seats. It was a long trip, but we didn't have a lot of money, so we slept on and off in our coach chairs. It wasn't so bad for Alma, because she was working as a saleslady in New York, and she was happy to be off her feet. I remember well that early in the morning the conductor told us to step out of the train at Deerfield Beach for a glass of fresh orange juice. All of this looked, as they say here, out of this world. That first sip was nothing less than ambrosia, especially after such a long journey. In my native Poland, orange juice was considered the most healthful beverage to drink. Even today, Alma carries home bags of oranges from the grocery store and squeezes glasses of fresh orange juice for breakfast each morning.

Someone told me the other day that a store in Miami Beach was giving out sample pieces of pineapple for free in the produce section. Can you imagine? Pineapple for free! Let me tell you, in Poland it was a custom on Rosh Hashanah that the rich would send gifts of pineapple, not a whole pineapple . . . just a slice. Such a slice cost 5 zlotys! And I tasted it once, and it had such a wonderful taste. Pineapple for free! It was then the highest luxury, and only on Rosh Hashanah to bring a blessing.

After we arrived at the train station in Miami, we took a taxi over the causeway to Miami Beach. As we rode over the causeway, I could hardly believe my eyes. It was almost unimaginable that in Miami Beach it was 80 degrees while in New York it was 20. Everything—the buildings, the water, the pavement—had an indescribable glow to it. The palm trees especially made a great impression on me. It was winter in New York, but when I came here I couldn't believe my own eyes, my own skin. It was really summer.

The driver let us off at the Pierre Motel where Alma had made reservations. It was owned by the brothers Gottlieb. I remember that a room there was seven dollars a day. To me this was a bit much. *Seven dollars a day!* Who can pay seven dollars a day? When I came they told me it was an especially good room, but then I saw a room for eight dollars a day that had a balcony, and I went and stood on that balcony and saw a palm tree. *Eight dollars a day!!!* In 1948 I was not a wealthy man; I barely made enough. But I looked out and saw a palm tree and I was very happy. Seven dollars a night was expensive, eight dollars a night was even more expensive.

I stayed at the Pierre and I stood on that balcony and stared at the palm tree in the yard for hours and hours. If someone had shown me a tree on which ten-dollar bills were growing, I could not have been more surprised. Let me tell you, to me when I came here the first time, I had a feeling that I had come to Paradise. First of all the palm trees. Where would I ever see a palm tree in my life? And the hotels were very beautiful. They still are.

I wrote articles for the *Jewish Daily Forward* on this trip, and the people were wondering . . . I described all this as if I had made a trip to Africa. I had discovered the palm tree. I told them my impressions about the palm trees, how they are like trees and not like trees, how different they are. They created a mood in me, and maybe in other people, too.

Alma would take me into all the hotels, just to see the lobby. You could go any day into the

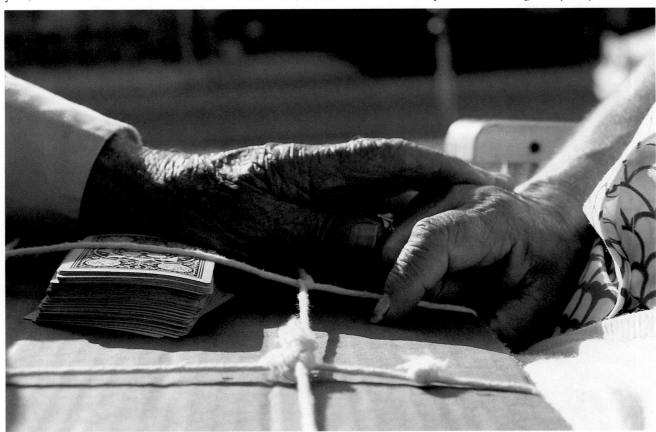

Park Scene   *February 1985*

vi

lobby of a hotel and just sit down. And I saw all kinds of people; I'd hear all kinds of Yiddish dialects. And by recognizing the Yiddish dialect, I could tell where they came from. And I saw them playing cards and making jokes that I had already heard many times before. And some were intimate and called each other "darling." Others acted like strangers. I saw again a piece of home.

It was remarkable: Jewishness had survived every atrocity of Hitler and his Nazis against the Jews. Here the sound of the Old World was as alive as ever. What I learned is that many people from the *shtetlach,* which I knew so well, came here, and some of them continued their love affairs. Somehow, the lovers came, and the he-lover and the she-lover, they went to New York and from New York to Miami. And I could see that what I wrote in my stories about the *shtetlach* happened right here. It continued right here. He still loves her although she's an old woman, and she loves him although he is an old man. They came together and talked and played cards. Miami Beach was a continuation of the little town.

For me, a vacation in Miami Beach was a chance to be among my own people. In those days Miami Beach was a magnet for Jewish people— a place where they flocked like geese to rest and warm themselves in the sun. In the 1940s and '50s, Miami Beach was in its so-called hey-day. It was a hub of Jewishness and a great source of inspiration for my stories. It was in those years at the Pierre and later at the Crown Hotel that I wrote chapters of *The Family Moskat,* my first big novel, which ran as a serial in *The Jewish Daily Forward.*

I came again year after year always to a hotel. I

stayed in almost all the hotels. I would often stay for four or five weeks. I even came in the summer a few times. It was so hot; there was no air conditioning yet, but I understood, if it's warm in the winter, it should be warmer in the summer. I even lived through a hurricane. From this experience I wrote the short story, "Alone." It is a summer story. I have written three other stories which use Miami Beach as a set-ting...."Old Love," "A Party in Miami Beach," and "The Hotel." "A Party in Miami Beach" is closest to how I feel about Miami Beach. I think this is a very important story, a humorous story. In "Old Love," I disguise my present apartment.

During the day, planes with long streamers flew over the beach advertising dinners with seven courses for $1.50 on Washington Avenue. There were a number of cafeterias. I like cafeterias be-cause I can meet people and hear them talk. They told me stories. Some recognized me as the writer for the *Forward* and they were eager to tell me more stories.

Rather than eat in the hotel (where Alma had trouble explaining to the *maitre d'* how to pre-pare a vegetarian meal for me), we often had dinner with acquaintances and old friends at one of the many cafeterias. We ate heartily:

Cafeteria, 20th and Collins Avenue   *February 1983*

Borscht, sweet-and-sour cabbage, mashed potatoes, salad, bread, coffee, and dessert.

The cafeterias were nostalgic places for me and I loved going to them. They reminded me of the Yiddish Writers Club in Warsaw, where I had rubbed elbows with not only some of the greatest Yiddish writers and poets but English and German as well, such as John Galsworthy and Hans Heinz Ewers. The same food was served and the same conversations took place. I noticed that often people met here again, after a long separation during the Hitler era, and a lot of tears of reunion were shed.

Miami Beach has changed a lot just from my memories. I used to walk a lot and it was all open beach. I used to walk from the Pierre to the Hotel Seagull for breakfast, and when we stayed at the Crown Hotel, after dinner, they would give away free tickets to a show at the Deauville. Once or twice a week they would stamp our wrists to show we had eaten dinner at the Crown. Now that was a big walk, but we could save the carfare.

For some reason we stopped coming to Miami Beach in the 1960s, but in 1973 I was invited

to give a lecture at Temple Beth Israel in downtown Miami. A former neighbor of Alma's in Munich, Mrs. Rosen, happened to come to my lecture. Afterward she invited us to her apartment on Collins Avenue in Surfside.

By then, we had fallen in love with Miami Beach all over again, and Mrs. Rosen suggested we buy an apartment in her building. The building was brand new and she had the key from the super so we could go all over the building and look at many apartments. We had a home in New York. Why did we need another apartment? Alma and I were sleepless for five days and nights struggling with the decision: Should we and could we afford to buy an apartment? In the middle of the night, we debated whether it was worth the high price. She reminded me that I was growing disgusted with New York; the air was so dusty and bad for my breathing. Finally the only decision I could make was to let my wife decide. In the end, we bought an apartment with a splendid view of the ocean where we live all year round today.

One block away is Sheldon's drugstore where Alma and I often have breakfast. One morning in 1978 I went to Sheldon's to have eggs and bagels. When I returned to the apartment after breakfast, Alma was calling out to me excitedly. Mr. Weber, my editor at the *Forward,* was on the telephone. He told me that he had heard on the transatlantic wire that I had won the Nobel Prize for literature. My hands grew completely cold, and Alma says I turned as white as a sheet.

But just because someone has won the Nobel Prize does not mean that life changes dramatically. After the ceremonies had ended and the interviews were over, life went on as before. Alma and I returned to our apartment on Col-

Issac and Alma at Sheldon's Drugstore   *March 1989*

typewriter, but it is getting very difficult to find parts when it needs repairs.

I was given a high honor. The street where Sheldon's is, is now Isaac Bashevis Singer Boulevard. They keep stealing the signs, but to be a living person and have a street named for you is a big honor.

They say Miami Beach will make a comeback, and who knows, maybe it will. Right now an exodus to Hollywood, Boca Raton and Fort Lauderdale is taking place. Nevertheless, for me, Miami Beach is still one of the most beautiful places in the world. Nothing can equal the splendor of nature. Every day, as I sit on the beach looking out at the ocean, each palm tree, each wave, each sea gull is still a great revelation to me. After fifteen years, Miami Beach feels like home.

lins Avenue, and I continued to write every day. I am still in the *Forward* every Friday. I am working on a serial novel called *The Secret* which takes place in New York and Brooklyn and the Bronx. And maybe Miami Beach, I haven't decided yet. I have a small desk in the bedroom that has good light, and I have a Yiddish

Isaac's Typewriter   *July 1990*
Isaac at Isaac Singer Boulevard   *January 1987*

Photographer's Note

My delight upon being introduced to Isaac and Alma Singer in Miami Beach soared when Isaac agreed to contribute an introduction to the photographic book I was developing. It was my hope that Isaac would provide some clues to the magnetic attraction Miami Beach held for his generation, and that through his words I could better understand the experiences of the many Eastern European immigrants I had met and photographed since my first trip to Miami Beach in 1979.

Isaac's illuminating essay, "My Love Affair with Miami Beach," emerged from our initial conversations in September 1986. With his consent, I borrowed this title for the book since it so aptly describes our mutual fascination with all that makes Miami Beach unique. As a second-generation American Jew, I felt that my photographic experiences were the closest I could get to breathing the air of the *shtetlach,* the small villages of Eastern Europe which are my roots. As Isaac says, "I could see what happened in my stories about the *shtetlach* happened right here. It continued right here."

A dialogue and friendship evolved in further conversations at Isaac and Alma's homes in Miami Beach and New York City. I found that many of his comments while viewing my images illuminated the issues raised by the photographs. It became clear to me that our dialogue would enhance and complement the images. With Isaac's gracious consent, I have used segments of our conversations in the manner of a Talmudic commentary which winds through the body of the photographs in this book. I am indebted to Isaac for generously contributing his wit and wisdom to my photographic journey through Miami Beach. And I am similarly indebted to Alma Singer for her friendship, assistance, and encouragement.

The photographs in this book are by no means an attempt to tell the full story of Miami Beach. Rather, they are an examination of the small Jewish neighborhood of South Beach. I visited dozens of times over a ten-year period to record a spirited community which survives while the forces of urban renewal and mortality threaten its existence. As of this writing (September 1990), the community is still alive in its stores, synagogues and hotels. But its days are clearly numbered; the Jewish population is declining and many of the locales in the photographs have been renovated or demolished. These photographs are an attempt to stop this flow of time, so that South Beach in the 1980s can fascinate, amuse, and enlighten forever.

—*R.N.*

CONVERSATIONS

Nagler: Isaac, I must say that I am very happy to have the opportunity to talk with you here in Miami Beach.

Singer: Oh, it's a great pleasure, and I hope that this talk will someday be a part of your book.

Nagler: Well, you speak for a generation, and you speak for many of the people I photograph. Many of the people I've met have been readers of yours for decades through your work in the *Jewish Daily Forward*. You've had a great sensitivity for the melodies and the rhythms of their lives.

Singer: Of course, I am one of them.

Nagler: When I mention your name, they often respond as if you are part of their family, and not just a famous author.

Singer: This is perhaps because I have revealed so much of myself to them. My work is highly auto-biographical.

Nagler: Isaac, I've read several interviews with you in which you indicate that, throughout your life, you seem to attract "strange" people. Miami Beach also has a reputation for a certain strangeness.

Singer: People in this country have a prejudice about Miami Beach; it means to them vulgar Jews. I say, "vulgar—shmulgar!" they're only people. When people are on vacation or they retire, they can act a little, as they say, "out of this world." I see many funny and silly things here often because many people desire to appear young and not old.

Nagler: You once said, "I am interested always in the exception—you might say, almost, in freaks. Because through the exception we can learn more about ourselves, about normal people."

Singer: When I meet people, I am never sure that I won't hear something about human nature or human character I have never heard before. People are always surprising me, and, maybe, I will put this person or a piece of this person into one of my stories.

(Previous page)
Conversation at the Deli   *November 1986*

Park Scene   *February 1980*

3

11th and Ocean Drive   *October 1986*

Beach Scene   *December 1984*

Nagler: Your stories remind me of so many people I have met while photographing down here. They are so similar in spirit. But what I've chosen to photograph are not the wealthy residents of the Miami Beach highrises, but the pensioners and what they call the "snowbirds," the ones who have settled or spend their winters in the original district.

Singer: You mean the old downtown, south of Lincoln Road?

Nagler: Exactly. It has come to be called South Beach.

Singer: I have stayed in many of the hotels in South Beach over the years. Each hotel was like a little village. But, it's not what it used to be anymore.
Lincoln Road was at one time a very beautiful shopping center. At one time it was called the Fifth Avenue of the South. It was then to me as today is the Bal Harbour Shopping Center, which is a place I often walk. Then it was right after the Depression, and I was amazed, as I still am today, to see the abundance in the store windows. Even though I am a man of very modest needs, I still like to look in the windows as if these things interested me.
And, of course, I hear little pieces of conversations and accents that may become part of a story.

Lobby, Primrose Hotel, 11th and Collins Avenue   *March 1985*

10th and Collins Avenue   *March 1985*

16th and Collins Avenue   *March 1988*

Nagler: It's fascinating for me to watch and photograph the lives of the old Jewish people who live down in South Beach, because, essentially, it's the end of an era. There really aren't any new Jews coming in except for the Hasidim who still come in the winter. The stores and the hotels that catered to this population are disappearing.

Singer: So if you want to see what old Jewish men look like, look at me.

Nagler: But you dress more like New York than Miami Beach.

Singer: Yes. That's true. Here you have eighty-year-old men dressing to look like fifteen-year-old boys. But, maybe that's right, because I have often said that an old man is nothing but a little boy.

Nagler: That reminds me of a description in your story, "A Party in Miami Beach." The narrator says, "I rode down in the elevator and saw a tiny man in a yellow shirt, green trousers, and violet shoes with gilt buckles."

Singer: That's the style of Miami Beach. You know the most peculiar thing is that they all try to be very young; they are so eager to appear young. Perhaps they try to convince themselves that here is the Fountain of Youth, that death will be confused by their clothes. We do get more oxygen here than in the mountains, that is sure. It's a good place to retire. Even an old gangster like Meyer Lansky needs a place to retire. And you cannot starve here, unless you don't have a penny, except on Yom Kippur.

Nagler: Do you fast on Yom Kippur?

Singer: Yes, I have this tradition that I fast. I once had in my life a Yom Kippur when I was already a free-thinker, and I wanted to eat to spite the Almighty. But I couldn't; I had nothing to eat. I was so poor that I couldn't afford food to eat. I had to fast. I said to the Almighty, "Okay, have it your way."

Street Scene, Collins Avenue   *February 1985*

11

9th and Ocean Drive   *February 1986*

12

8th and Ocean Drive   *December 1990*

13

Singer: I'm glad you read "A Party in Miami Beach." I have published four stories about Miami Beach in various anthologies, but "A Party in Miami Beach" is the most humorous one, and the one which is the closest to how I feel about Miami Beach.

Nagler: There's a character in "A Party in Miami Beach" who comes up to you at a cocktail party, and says, "If my parents wanted to say something I wouldn't understand, they spoke Yiddish." And that's how it was in my family, too. It was a secret language for many in my generation.

Singer: Yes, and I hear this a million times. Every time I give, let's say, a lecture, people come over and tell me the same thing. But, actually, it is not a language to keep secrets from little children. It is a special language, rich in description of human character and human personality. So, it is more than that, more than a language for spies.

Nagler: One of the attractions of South Beach for me is that I encounter many people for whom Yiddish is still a primary means of communication. I have photographed groups of people singing Yiddish songs on the beach, or telling stories in the hotels at night. You've said that Yiddish is a very sensual language . . .

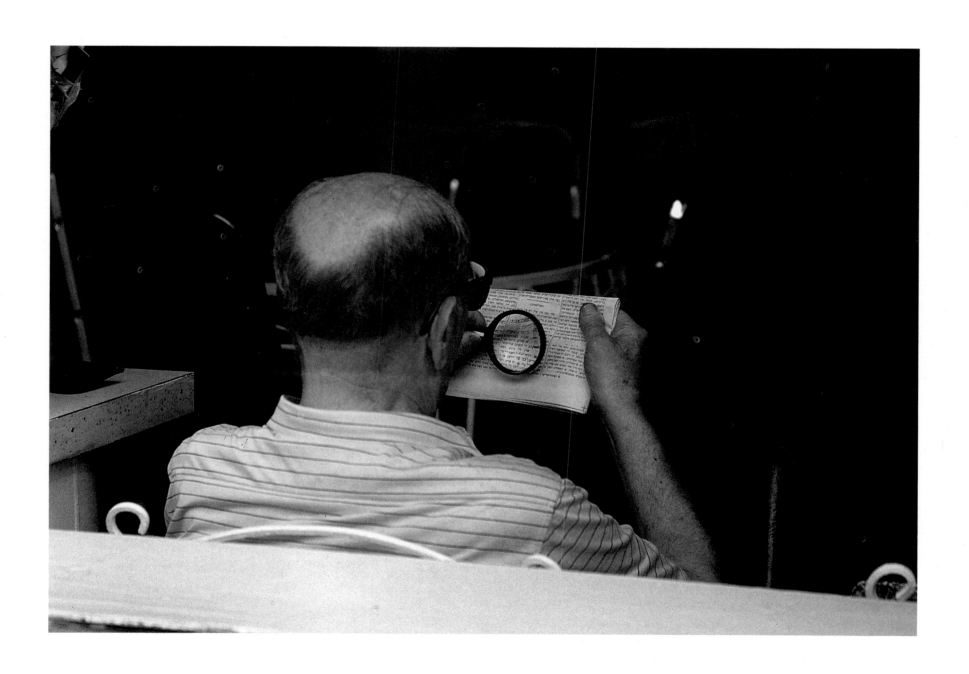

Street Scene, Washington Avenue   *March 1988*

Park Scene   *February 1986*

16

11th and Collins Avenue   *March 1987*

17

Singer: I've said that Yiddish has a lot of vitamins. What I mean is that Yiddish has the ability to convey the zest of life, if the writer has the power. In my case, since I write mostly about Yiddish speaking people, I write in the language my protagonist speaks. Yiddish is a language that has many idioms that give zest to the language; it is a language rich in idioms. Let me tell you that the Yiddish language is not rich in, let's say, technology. If I would want to write a book about the atomic bomb and describe it all in Yiddish, I would have a lot of difficulties with it. But Yiddish is immensely rich in describing human character. You can say that there are maybe a hundred words in Yiddish about "a poor man." There are all kinds of words and each means a little different. And the same is true about "a stingy man," or "a loose woman," or "a pious woman." When it comes to describe a character, Yiddish is immensely rich. But when it comes to describing architecture or cars or such things, Yiddish is poor. But if I have to describe something technological, I manage. I take English words, or I take words from German. Sometimes I make up words by myself; I can create a word. I don't indulge in it, but a writer has the right every once in a while to create a word. I'd rather take ready-made words than create new ones.

Nagler: In my walks around South Beach, I have met many people who are parallel to what you are describing about Yiddish. They are very untechnological. They're not electronic people, but they have a great zest for life. They love to sit and talk. A good conversation is very important; stories are very important. Dances are well-attended. I imagine that it can sound like a Polish or Russian village. I hear Yiddish folksongs. I hear balalaikas and mandolins.

Singer: It's there. It's there.

10th and Ocean Drive   *November 1988*

19

Park Scene   *February 1984*

9th and Ocean Drive   *February 1984*

Nagler: When I photograph in South Beach, I often sense what you allude to in your writings, about when as a child you went to visit Bilgoray, your mother's small village in Poland. There you could feel the movement of Jewish history through the ages.

Singer: Yes, Bilgoray often appears in my writing as a time that is no more, but my childhood years in Warsaw were the most important to my writing. My childhood is to me like a gold mine where I can always dig for treasure. I have returned many times to Number 10 Krochmalna Street where I lived as a little boy in Warsaw. It was there that I was introduced to the whole richness of human character. I can still remember conversations I overheard there as if they were yesterday.
I cannot answer if there was something special about the *shtetl* experience, because it was the only life I have known, but, somehow for me, it is easier to go back to Warsaw in my memories than any other time in my life. I met many saints and sinners—and sometimes they were the same person.

Three Generations, New Year's Eve, 11th and Collins Avenue   *December 1987*

23

Congregation Knesseth Israel   *February 1989*

Beach Scene   *February 1985*

Nagler: Isaac, I wanted to show you this photograph I took of two young Hasidic boys . . . best friends.

Singer: Where did you take this?

Nagler: Their families were staying at the Essex House Hotel at 10th and Collins where many Hasidim come during the winter for a vacation. It has taken me many years to build up trust among the Hasidim so that many are now comfortable with me taking their pictures. Of course, there are some very strict Hasidim who will not permit photography at all.

Singer: And the parents of these boys didn't mind?

Nagler: No, many people have come to accept me over the years. I've sent many people photographs and I try to keep up a correspondence. I try to demonstrate to them that my motive is one of respect and not profit. Many of the people to whom I've sent pictures have offered to pay me, but I always indicate that it's my pleasure, that it's what I like to do.

Singer: You know, I might have looked exactly like these boys. There are no pictures of me as a child, but I have seen pictures of my great-grandchild in Israel, and I see in those pictures as I see in this photograph what is, I believe, my own face.

Street Scene   *February 1986*

Nagler: I know from your writing that you were raised in an Hasidic environment. Was there a specific injunction against painting or photographing the human figure?

Singer: Yes. This is in the Ten Commandments: "Thou shalt not make any images." Because image making was connected with idolatry. Where you had an image, it meant you served this image. It became kind of a god or took the place of God. Also, the fact is when you did this, you did not study the holy books. You took away time from prayer and study and gave it to worldly things. From a religious point of view, especially from a Jewish religious point of view, a person should do good deeds and study the Talmud. Whatever else you did, there's no reason for it.

Nagler: I know your brother was a freethinker and became an artist in Warsaw. When you went to visit his studio, did you first see people painting the human figure?

Singer: Yes, yes. As a matter of fact, I saw there some girls who took off their blouses. Some of them wanted to be painted half-naked and naked. I considered it very terrible. It was a sin, but it also attracted me.

Beach Scene   *February 1990*

Nagler: The dialectic between saintliness and sinfulness has always been a strong undercurrent in your work. I presume you appeared to be a typical Hasidic little boy when you went to your brother's studio.

Singer: Yes, I had *peyes*, what they call earlocks, and I dressed mostly in black. But I was unusual in that I had blue eyes, red hair, and white, white skin. The artists and models, however, were quite modern in appearance. Most of these girls looked more or less like girls today. In the time after World War I, short dresses became very fashionable—short dresses and short hair for girls, and they all wore dresses up to their knees.

My brother's friends who were painters and sculptors always wanted me to sit for a portrait, and all these girls would try to tease me playfully. Here I was this little Hasid boy with blue eyes and red hair, but I was too frightened. I wanted to go back because my mother was always worried when she sent me to my brother's with food. I never stayed too long there.

Let me tell you, when I was a boy visiting my brother's studio, I thought that breasts were something that only a married woman has. It never occurred to me that a girl should have breasts. Because I only saw breasts when a woman was nursing her baby, so she was a married woman. And when I finally saw a girl with breasts, I was flabbergasted! I said to my brother, "Is she married? Does she have a child? No child! Then where did she get breasts?" All right, I made a mistake.

Beach Scene   *February 1990*

31

Nagler: Many times before I go out to take photographs in Miami Beach, I will look at books of Chagall paintings. It's my hope that by trying to connect with Chagall's imagery, I'll be able to get a better understanding of what the *shtetl* might have looked like, or felt like to him in Russia. For instance, on this trip, I've been trying to mimic Chagall by taking some pictures underwater. I'm hoping to parody the feeling of levitation that characterizes many Chagall paintings. On previous trips, I've tried to use the sandblasted windows in some of old hotels to form backgrounds where fish and birds dance and float behind people. Less successful for me was a period of long exposures at night where, once again, the hope was to achieve a more surreal quality.

Singer: People always try to put me in the same boat with Chagall. When they ask me, I say, "Chagall was Chagall, and I am I." I don't write like Chagall paints. Chagall doesn't paint like I write. And as a matter of fact, he gave the same answer. There are parallels because we are both attached to a way of life which has disappeared or is disappearing. But things don't disappear very quickly. There will still be Hasidim a hundred years from now, I assure you. They will wear these long robes still. Even in Miami Beach. So it's a little hot, so what?

Pool at Tropics Hotel, 15th and Collins Avenue   *October 1986*

9th and Collins Avenue   *January 1990*

Primrose Hotel, 11th and Collins Avenue   *December 1984*

Nagler: Let me read you a quote from your book, *In My Father's Court*, in which you describe Bilgoray, your mother's village to which you moved from Warsaw. This quotation has grown to symbolize for me what I seek in my photography in Miami Beach: "In this world of old Jewishness I found a spiritual treasure trove. I had the chance to see our past as it really was. Time seemed to flow backwards. I lived Jewish history."
When I look at a Chagall painting, I often have this feeling, too. And that's why I feel such a great debt to you and Chagall in my photography. You once said, "Only small fish swim in schools." To me you and Chagall are two big fish—two great talents who created unique styles in your respective fields.

Singer: Oh thank you. You are most kind to say so. I would say every human being is himself or herself. Life cannot be an imitation; people wouldn't compare you to other people. No comparison could really do justice to you or the other people. You are you and they are they.

Nagler: Here's another picture where I really had Chagall on my mind. I went back to this barbershop at least three times over the years, because I wanted to capture an image where the reflections from the mirror floated behind the people. I learned a little from each visit. It's a barbershop on Washington Avenue called the Times Square Barbershop . . .

Singer: Times Square in Miami Beach!

Nagler: And I think this image successfully conveys the beauty of the Friday afternoon haircut ritual and the tenderness of the relationship between the barber and his customer.

Singer: Yes, it looks very good.

Nagler: When I went back to the barbershop on the following visit, the store was empty. The man next door told me that the barber had become ill. There were no signs that a barbershop had ever existed there.

Times Square Barbershop, 9th and Washington Avenue   *March 1985*

Washington Avenue Barbershop   *January 1990*

Hollywood Beauty Salon, 12th and Washington Avenue   *March 1989*

Singer: Tell me, Richard, did you photograph yesterday?

Nagler: It never fails that when I'm in Miami Beach, I see interesting things to photograph. Yesterday, even though I had just gotten in after a long flight, as I got to my room in the hotel . . .

Singer: To what hotel did you go?

Nagler: I was at The Clevelander, and, incidentally, it felt like I was the only one in the hotel, a lot like your story, "Alone." Before I had a chance to unpack or change clothes, I happened to look out the window, and this was Sunday evening at sundown, and I saw a group of men in suits, carrying prayer books, and walking out to the beach. It must have been 90 degrees, the middle of an autumn heat wave. I was wearing a sweater and heavy pants, because it had been cool in San Francisco, but I grabbed a camera and ran down to find out what was going on.

Singer: Saturday was Rosh Hashanah. Because the New Year fell on a Saturday this year, they were going to *tashlik.*

Nagler: *Tashlik.* Yes, that's right, that's what a man told me. I had never heard of it, and I had never seen people on the beach in prayer before. I was told by some nice gentlemen that this was a special prayer which is only done at Rosh Hashanah.

Singer: I wrote a story once called "Tashlik." It's in the book called *Stories for Children.* You throw into the ocean or the river all the sins from the previous year. It is because there is a passage in the Bible where God says, "And you will throw into the ocean all your sins."
In Poland we could not go to the ocean, so we would go to the Vistula every year. Any body of water will do.

Beach Scene, Rosh Hashanah   *September 1986*

41

Street Scene, Purim   *March 1988*

Street Scene, Chanukah   *December 1989*

Singer: Do you have these photographs of *tashlik*? Will they be published in your book?

Nagler: You never know until you see the photograph, and that takes time, whether it successfully conveys the power or beauty of the experience. This morning I photographed a man while we floated together in the ocean. He told me that he had been a pants presser for forty-seven years in New Jersey. The work was very, very hard, but especially summers, the heat was unbearable. He managed to put two children through college and he was now retired in Miami Beach. He was very proud and not bitter. He told me that although life was hard, that he had an expression in Yiddish that sustained him. He said it in Yiddish and then translated it for me as: "Only with sweat will you have bread."

Singer: Yes, yes. It's from the Bible: "From the sweat of your face will you have bread." It's from the book of Genesis: "And God cursed Adam and Eve for eating from the tree of knowledge." He cursed them with these words, "With the sweat of your brow you eat."

Ocean Scene   *October 1986*

Beach Scene   *February 1990*

46

Pool, Sagamore Hotel, Collins Avenue and Lincoln Road   *March 1987*

47

Nagler: A few years back, I took this photograph of men in prayer about 8:00 one Saturday morning outside the Essex House Hotel. The art-deco architectural feature above the men in their prayer shawls is called an "eyebrow." So, I've come to call this image, "The Eye of God." The eyebrow is above, the windows represent the eye itself, and if you look inside the eye—the window— you'll see an old man sitting in prayer.

Singer: Yes, I see him . . . a very, very old man. Is he still alive?

Nagler: By way of answer, let me say that I read an interview you gave once in which you said that literature is your way of cheating death. Once you create a character, give it a name, it lives forever.

Singer: Yes, in a way, because this character will live in literature longer than he ever could have lived in real life. I hope so, anyhow.

Nagler: That's a clue to my photography, also. I feel that photography helps cheat death a little bit, like your literature.

Singer: Of course, because these people were alive when you made the picture; they are still alive. Ten years later, they are gone, but their images are still with you. Their faces express the same feelings as they expressed then. Photography is a very, very important invention. I would say that photography and the telephone are the two most important inventions of technology. Photography is important because it takes a minute and makes it an eternity. And so goes art, if it's right.

10th and Collins Avenue   *February 1984*

Congregation Beth Jacob   *February 1990*

Congregation Knesseth Israel   *March 1989*

51

Nagler: Often when I photograph here, I think of a quote from your book, *In My Father's Court*. Let me remind you of this paragraph: "My father began to talk to me about the Lamed Vov—the thirty-six hidden saints—the simple Jews, the tailors, shoemakers, and water carriers upon whom depends the continued existence of the world. Father spoke of their poverty, their humility, their appearance of ignorance so that none would recognize their true greatness. He spoke of these concealed saints with a special love, and he said, 'One contrite heart is of greater worth before the Almighty than thirty silk gaberdines.' " Could you tell me a bit more about the concept of the Lamed Vov?

Singer: It really isn't a concept or a story. It's a belief. It's not from the Bible or the Talmud. It could be that the Lamed Vov are first mentioned in the Midrash. It has since become almost more like a legend, this is clear. Lamed Vov means literally "thirty-six." It is one of several legends that have served to give the people hope at times in history when things were so hard for the Jews. The Lamed Vov are always out in the world trying to do good, trying to help people, but we can never know who they truly are. They do not reveal themselves. Without them the Earth falls to pieces and spins out of control. They seem like ordinary people, and we call people who aspire to do good, to be like them, Lamed Vovniks.
Like the coming of the Messiah, the Lamed Vov tell us that there are only a small minority of people who make life in the world worth living.

Nagler: I am trying to find and record this quality, a gentleness and saintliness, in the people I am photographing in Miami Beach.

Singer: There are such people . . . quite a number. But as for the Lamed Vov, you want to photograph them? You won't find it here. But go on making more pictures. Maybe by accident you will take a picture of a true Lamed Vov saint. And maybe if you make a good picture of one, he may reveal himself to you.

Garden of Eden Fruit Store, 5th and Washington Avenue   *February 1990*

Beach Scene   *January 1990*

Hotel Senator, 12th and Collins Avenue   *February 1984*
(Demolished October 1988)

9th and Ocean Drive   *February 1985*

9th and Ocean Drive   *March 1987*

57

Nagler: I had a sad experience the other night when I went to find one of my favorite Lamed Vovniks. I went to visit a woman I have photographed many times over the years at the park down at the beach. She was most often sitting by herself, listening to the radio . . . a tiny lady always looking like a jewel. I liked her instantly. When you first meet some people and ask to take their picture, they can be frightened . . .

Singer: Suspicious?

Nagler: . . . or afraid. A camera can be like a gun to some people. But this woman was the opposite. The minute I started talking to her, she blossomed like a flower.

Singer: I should think most people would be like that. Where did she come from?

Nagler: She came from Russia, and she came to the United States at age thirteen with only her brother who was fourteen. Her parents, because of the pogroms, managed to scrape together the money to send them away. She remembered coming home one day to her *shtetl* and finding her parents crushed because a horrible thing had happened. Her older sister had been raped and murdered. Whoever committed this terrible crime, had, as a final act, cut off her sister's breasts. The next day was the last she saw her parents.
There I was, on a beautiful day in Miami Beach, talking to this little jewel of a person, being reminded of the horrors many in your generation experienced. She told me this story without rancor, but with a weary sadness in her voice.
She told me that after getting to the United States, where she knew no one, for many years she kept writing to her parents in Russia, but she never heard a word back.

Singer: They didn't let them write. In my time to go to America, it was almost like dying. There was an expression that over the ocean is almost like in the cemetery. When they accompanied the people to the trains which took them to the ships, they were crying. The parents knew that they would never see the children again, because it happened very seldom that they came back. People used to go to Israel also in those old times, which incidentally was a longer trip than to America, and when someone went there he was already considered dead.

9th and Ocean Drive   *February 1986*

Hotel Primrose, 11th and Collins Avenue   *January 1987*

Hotel Plymouth, 21st and Park   *February 1986*

Nagler: I went to her apartment because I wanted to tape record the history she had told me. I had looked for her earlier, expecting to see her as I always did down at the park, but she wasn't there. I rang her bell. An Hispanic woman answered, but she didn't speak English. I found the building super who told me that about six months ago, my friend had taken a bad fall. She was in her late eighties and now she was in a nursing home. Her daughter had come down and closed up the apartment.
Unfortunately, the super was a very suspicious type and wouldn't give me the name of the nursing home or the daughter's address.

Singer: Perhaps this lady had died.

Nagler: All I know is that she had fallen and cut her face badly. And I was told that her mind was affected. That's why I feel I must take these photographs now, because . . .

Singer: Yes, of course!

Nagler: There are certain time limitations that we cannot transcend.

Singer: Of course, of course. You know I still believe in God, but my feeling for the Almighty is coupled with a great anguish of protest and pessimism. I am optimistic that God has a plan for the Universe, but I am pessimistic that He is an eternally silent God who may not ever reveal this plan to us. Once I told an interviewer that, if I could, I would protest in front of God with a sign that said: "Unfair to Life."
All I can say is that to me the best way to serve God is to be nice to other human beings. If you are not being nice to another human being, you are insulting God.

Nursing Home, 9th and Ocean Drive   *March 1988*

63

Judaica Store, 13th and Washington Avenue   *March 1989*

Washington Avenue Barbershop   *January 1988*

Nagler: Issac, you once said in regard to your writing, "Since I often describe people like myself and I am interested in human ideas, I let my people ponder the eternal questions. I could never make the protagonist of a novel a person who would not be interested in those questions." Today I would like to talk to you about those eternal questions, which, I think, bear relevance to the work I'm doing here.

Singer: Yes, absolutely. Take your time. Take your time.

Nagler: Many of my photographs from South Beach are disturbing to people because they deal directly with aging and mortality.

Singer: Let me tell you, I always felt that there is really no difference, no basic difference, between young and old. The difference is not so large as people think. Because when you are born, you have already all the qualities of yourself, of your being, readymade. They were done in your mother's belly. And if you are a pessimist, you were already a pessimist in your mother's belly. And if you are an optimist, the same thing is true, too. And the same thing is true in every way. Because of this, I would say, from the cradle to the grave, we are the same. As a matter of fact, there is a Yiddish expression: "What you take out from the cradle you put into the grave."
So, because of this, although I remember everything which happened to me, many things which happened to me in my life, and I remember many silly things, but I understand all this because I know that I was then the same as what I am today. Of course, there is some development, but the genes, the genes are with us from the very beginning to the very end.
As for me, when I was born, I asked the midwife, "Where is my secretary?" All my life, I can never find anything.

11th and Collins Avenue   *January 1988*

Handball Players, Flamingo Park, 7:30 AM   *March 1985*

Park Scene, 12th and Ocean Drive   *January 1990*

Nagler: So at times, do you still feel like an Hasidic schoolboy with long *peyes*?

Singer: Of course. My enemies from the school, the *cheder,* whether they are dead or whatever happened to them, I still have some calculations with them. I still remember little insults and little struggles and good things we had together. It's the same thing with women in my life. It's always there; nothing is really lost.

Nagler: It's important for me at this point in my life to confront questions regarding aging and mortality. These are concerns that I try to address in my photographs. I look to these images for clues. And certainly Miami Beach is for me a place where there are many experiences that cause me to continue to question. Maybe there's something in a face that will help me.

Singer: No, we don't know the answers. Even if we would know, we wouldn't want to know. All I can say is, when I see you, I could very well describe you as a little boy in school. I would know more or less what you would say. Of course, I would make of you a Yiddish-speaking boy, but you would still be the same.

Essex House Hotel, 10th and Collins Avenue   *February 1986*

Nagler: Yesterday at lunch you spoke to me so passionately about your belief in God.

Singer: Yes, I do believe in God. I don't think that the world is an accident, that a few molecules met by some accident and then they combined and they created human beings. Even scientists today move away more and more from Darwin, because the facts show that there was a plan to all this; it was not just an accident. It was not just a big bang which created the universe; before the big bang was created, a universe was potentially already there.
I have always believed that there is a higher power, and that there is a plan to all this which is not revealed to us. What I call God is, I believe, the authority for all this planning. God for me means the plan of the world. I just cannot believe that all that we see and feel is the result of some cosmic accident.
My God is a silent God, who leaves us alone to make our choices during our days. Just the same, at times, I wish He would reveal Himself to man and say this is the way to behave, this is what to do. And yet, at other times, I am full of doubt, like an uncertain lover.
I am not sure that my belief in God helps me as I get older, but it does help to a degree. If you lose, let's say your wallet or twenty dollars, you are just as much in despair as if you would have been a poor man. Being rich in philosophy does little for anguish or despair. You cannot use your philosophy. But as much as I can, I use it. I say to myself that my little troubles are not troubles of the universe, or, if they are, they have to be like this. You get some comfort from your religion. But only some, not enough.

Congregation Etz Chaim   *November 1988*

73

Street Scene, 3rd and Washington Avenue   *February 1983*

74

Street Scene   *March 1985*

75

Singer: If you look about in our society today, you will see the consequences of men who do not have a belief in higher powers. For thousands of years in human history, men believed that there was a God or gods. Today there is much unhappiness and disappointment, and because of these feelings of great despair, we live in a world where people seek solace with drugs. This century has seen two wars on a global scale along with the rise of Hitler and Stalin. It is a difficult age to sustain one's beliefs; God's mercy seems more and more difficult to find.

My father was a pious man of the highest order. He used to say that reading a newspaper in the morning was like eating poison for breakfast. By that he meant he did not need to know anything about the world of men. He had his religion and he had his hope in the coming of the Messiah. God gave us the Torah and the Talmud and these books hold the key to our lives. This was his faith.

Today, there are many with no faith at all, and no belief in their free choices, and so they are content to eat poison.

10th and Collins Avenue, Sabbath   *March 1987*

Handball Players, Flamingo Park   *January 1990*

Washington Avenue   *November 1988*

Nagler: Are you angry at God for how little knowledge He's given us?

Singer: I'm angry not only for the little knowledge, but for so much trouble He has given us. I think no matter what His excuses are, I cannot forgive Him completely for seeing the Nazis put children into the gas chambers, you know. But we are not here really to forgive God. We have completely the right to be angry with Him, to say to Him, "It is true that you are great and we are small. It is true that you have all the information and we have almost nothing. Just the same, what you did to all the victims, what you did to us, is not forgivable, cannot be forgiven."

Nagler: Your answer reminds me of something you once said in an interview: "Actually our knowledge is a little island in an infinite ocean of non-knowledge. And even this little island remains a riddle."

Singer: Of course, of course it is. Ach, we know almost nothing. You have to take it as it comes. What can we do?

Nagler: Human nature is very complicated. I have photographed a concentration camp survivor who said "I like to live," and another who said, "I don't want to talk about myself. Sometimes it's better to say nothing. It only makes me sad. I've had a hard life. Some people are born with luck; I was not."

Congregation Lubavitch, South Beach Chabad   *March 1987*

11th and Ocean Drive   *October 1986*

82

Lobby, Breakwater Hotel, 10th and Ocean Drive *February 1986*

83

Nagler: I'm sitting here looking out your window at the beach, and I'm thinking of the statement that scientists always make so flippantly; they say, "Well, if you added up all the grains of sand on the beach, you still wouldn't equal the number of stars in the universe..."

Singer: Of course, of course. We cannot understand eternity; we cannot understand endlessness. We know that they exist, but we cannot really live with that.

Nagler: That's why I loved your character, Max Flederbush, the businessman in "A Party in Miami Beach." All he wanted to know was how much a condominium was going to cost in Miami Beach in 10,000 years. That's all he needed to know about the future.

Singer: (*Laughing*) Yeah, and there is a character in this story, the humorist, Kazarsky, I think, who answers "a trillion dollars."

Nagler: I have it here... "a condominium with one bedroom for the fish will cost five trillion dollars." And then Max asks, "And what will be in New York? In Paris? In Moscow? Will there still be Jews?" And Kazarsky answers, "There will be only Jews." "What kind of Jews?" asks Max. "Crazy Jews just like you."

Singer: I'm glad you like this story. I felt that you would have to read this story, because it would do a lot for your book. "A Party in Miami Beach" feels to me like a small piece of the crazy world here. Do you agree?

Nagler: It's a great story, but the story that touches me the most and feels closest to what I photograph is "The Hotel."

Singer: Ah, yes, "The Hotel" is more about people I see than about myself. It is a story about compulsion. They had to buy the hotel or they would die.

Wolfie's Restaurant, 21st and Collins Avenue   *March 1988*

5th and Ocean Drive　　　　*March 1988*

Beach Scene   *February 1990*

Park Scene   *March 1988*

11th and Ocean Drive   *March 1988*

Nagler: Speaking of "A Party in Miami Beach," you're 82 now as we speak, and we're in a city where there are many elderly Jewish people, many aging Eastern European Jews. This is a little difficult for me to address, so I'll use the words of your character, Max Flederbush, "Here you can forget about death as much as you can forget to breathe."

Singer: Many of my friends, my school friends and my girlfriends from the *cheder*, are all dead. But my calculations with them, my feelings about them, are the same as on the first day of our meeting. I do not think of them as being dead. To me they are alive.

Nagler: So when you look at a photograph of yourself, do you see the school boy, do you see the Warsaw journalist, or do you see the eighty-two-year-old man?

Singer: I see the *cheder* boy at this moment. I feel that if you had been there, had come to interview me, I would most probably have told you the same things I am saying today, or near to the same things.
I have often said that my future is my past. By that I mean that I live with the stories in the Book of Genesis...
Rachel, Jacob. They are to me the most living people. And I remember things that happened to me in my childhood better than things that happened to me yesterday.
And as for death, I was thinking about it when I was twelve years old already. Whenever I read in a newspaper or in a book about sickness, immediately I thought I had it. I was a kind of hypochondriac.
And I will tell you, there were funerals on Krochmalna street all the time. And I saw women go after the hearses, crying and demanding justice, and lifting up their fists to heaven and moaning, "Ach, why did you do this? What has he done?" or, "What did she do?"
People think that in this country death is a mystery because it happens behind closed doors. There death happened everywhere and it was still a great mystery; it is a mystery everywhere. People get sick; some live longer, some shorter. No one really knows.

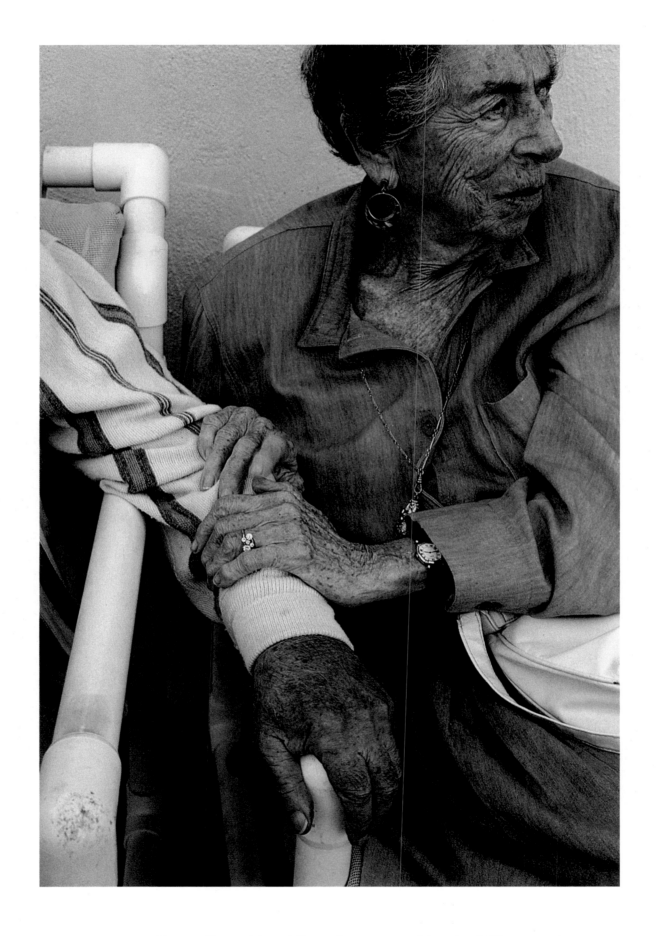

Nursing Home, 9th and Ocean Drive   *November 1988*

7th and Washington Avenue   *February 1984*

Street Scene, 10th and Collins Avenue   *February 1986*

93

Nagler: In 1944, your brother, who was also a writer, died suddenly. You have said that this was a terrible point in your life.

Singer: Ach, this was the tragedy of my existence. When this happened to me, I said to myself nothing can ever happen to me that is worse than that. At least I've reached a summit to my misery. There is a crisis in every human life. If you meet a person, you can say without knowing that there has been a crisis in their life.
My brother was a highly ethical human being. He died so unexpectedly. The evening before he died, I met him in a restaurant with his wife. And we talked and we joked. In the morning my wife, Alma, came to tell me the bitter news. I felt that God has given me a slap in the face. But what could I do? Give him a slap back? It was very hard, but I had to go on. I always had to wonder why my brother was taken and not me. It created in me a feeling of guilt. Why wasn't I better to him? Why didn't I come to him every hour of the day? You know I had the feeling that many may have, that we neglected the most important thing in our life. This feeling is beyond correction.

Brothers, Park Scene   *March 1985*

95

Sisters, 8th and Ocean Drive   *February 1984*

Sisters, 12th and Collins Avenue   *February 1986*

Nagler: I photographed a man the other day who seemed as old as you can possibly be.

Singer: Most probably 95 or something.

Nagler: I could see every vein in his arm. But, coincidentally, last year, I had photographed this same person walking down Ocean Avenue. I remember thinking the same thought then, that this has got to be as old as you can get. Yet, there he was again the other day, six months later. I was so glad to see him.

Singer: Last year I met a man whose boarder I was in Seagate, in Brooklyn, when I first came to this country in the 1930s. And he was already 102 or 104, over the hundred quite a lot. And I asked him, I said, "What do you think now, after all these years?" He said it wasn't worth it. "I would have been better off if I hadn't been born," more or less is what he said to me. And he was quite a clever man—a simple man and a clever man.

Nagler: On a previous trip I photographed a man of 102, whose attitude was very different. Although he's blind, every day he walks the few blocks to the bandstand at 9th and Ocean Drive to sing a few songs. The other singers are mostly in their eighties, so he's kind of a celebrity amongst them; they're all very proud of him. Once he told me, "The women try to make a play for me, but when they hear my age, they drop me like a hot potato."

Singer: I'm like him. I still have my work. And I have more stories to tell.

9th and Ocean Drive   *February 1986*

1st and Ocean Drive   *February 1980*

Viewer at Photography Exhibition, Bass Museum, 21st and Park   *February 1983*

101

Street Scene, Ocean Drive   *February 1980*

104

11th and Pennsylvania Avenue   *November 1988*

105

Nagler: If I had said to the schoolboy in Poland, "Someday you're going to be living your life by a beautiful ocean, by a beautiful beach, where you will never have a cold winter again . . ."

Singer: I will tell you one thing. In Poland, when you went to the stores, they used to pack the herring or whatever, the cheese, into paper. Where did they get the paper? They'd get old newspapers from Sweden, from Germany, from other countries. So they used to pack my herring into a newspaper, and sometimes it was in English. And I said to myself, "This language I'm going to know one day." I don't know why, but I felt something when I looked at the English words, that this looked to me like a real language, which attracted me.
Of course, there was no clue that someday I would know the language, but I always had this feeling that there is something in this language which is somehow near to me. In a way, we foresee partially the future. Not always. Or we get a notion about it.

Nagler: As for the future, do you think that there will ever be a generation that experiences change such as that which has occurred in your lifetime?

Singer: I will tell you, we don't always know what the future will bring. This is prophecy. We don't know. Of course there are changes all the time. Human conditions keep on changing, and, of course, there will be writers who will take care of these changes, who will be interested in them. Whether the 21st century is going to be like the 20th, no one can really know. Most probably the changes will be so surprising and so unusual that those who live through them will be all the time astonished. But, still, life is full of surprises, and so is literature, you know.

Street Scene, 7th and Ocean Drive   *November 1988*

Hotel Senator, 12th and Collins Avenue   *February 1984*
(Demolished October 1988)

Street Scene   *February 1990*

Street Scene   *March 1988*

Street Scene   *March 1984*

111

Nagler: You were born just one year after the Wright brothers first flew at Kitty Hawk. Now, due to modern air travel, you could decide to go anywhere on the Earth and be there comfortably within twenty-four hours. Man first flew and walked on the moon during your lifetime.

Singer: You cannot really be astonished all the time. The 19th century had many changes, too. When I was born there already was the telephone, also the automobile and electricity. I know that things have changed and I make allowances. I'm sure that if I lived another ten years there would be more surprises. Not that I expect it, but it could happen.

And who can say that there will not be future generations in which even greater changes will occur. But actually, with all the changes, human beings remain the same.

In a way, my books tell the history of the 20th century. But I also go back in some of my stories to the 19th or the 18th. In some of them I go back to the 17th century, like *The Slave.*

You see, the reason that I'm able to write about these other centuries is because I heard so many stories, and I met so many old people, that I am connected somehow with many generations before me.

As for Poland, and Warsaw, and the *shtetl,* it is true that for me it is still sometimes as if I live there. Even though we are talking today in Miami Beach, in the United States, my orientation and my feelings are still a result of the first thirty years of my life in Poland. I have told you that, for me as a writer, the Poland of my youth still exists. You could say I have one foot here and one foot there.

Lobby, Hotel Tiffany, 8th and Collins Avenue   *February 1986*

Miami Beach Post Office, 12th and Washington Avenue   *December 1989*

Lobby, Hotel Plymouth, 21st and Park   *February 1986*

Nagler: Given all we've been talking about, Isaac, this may be the appropriate time for me to take a portrait of you.

Singer: Surely. Just say so. Since you are the boss; this is what photographers are. You can move the ceiling if you want.
They say to me, "Look up, look down, look away, to the left, to the right," then they say, "Be completely natural."

Nagler: Well, I'll try to be a bit more gentle. I've been thinking a lot about how I'd like to photograph you, and the setting that occurs to me is of you, at this stage of your life, on a balcony with the ocean behind you. As I read your work, I have noticed that you often use a balcony as a literary device from which you can observe human foibles from a detached perspective. Also, quite often, it is on a balcony that you or your characters ponder those "eternal questions" which we spoke about before.
I mentioned earlier that great quote from *Lost in America*, but there's another great balcony scene from *My Father's Court* that comes to mind. You are still a child in the book when you say, "I stood on the balcony in my satin gaberdine and my velvet hat, and gazed about me. How vast was this world, and how rich in all kinds of people and strange happenings! And how high was the sky above the rooftops! And how deep the earth beneath the flagstones! And why did men and women love each other? And where was God, who was constantly spoken of in our house? I was amazed, delighted, entranced. I felt that I must solve this riddle, I alone, with my own understanding."

Singer: Come, let's step outside.

Portrait of Isaac Bashevis Singer   *October 1986*

Acknowledgments

This book would not be in your hands if it weren't for the significant roles played by Peter Beren and Dvorah Menashe. I thank them both. I also thank Isaac and Alma Singer for letting me enter their fascinating and enlightening universe.

I am fortunate to have had the support, encouragement, and assistance of many friends over the years. I would like to express particular gratitude to Denis Clifford, Naomi Puro, Patricia Mitchell, David Marell, Ellen and Michael Starr, Jeffrey and Donna Jaffee, Larry Press, Dale Pollock, Mark Liszt, Karyl Sisson, Jane Staw, Hugh and Nancy Brady, Fran van Bergen, Frish Brandt and Michael Shapiro. My brother Lanny Nagler, a fine photographer, was inspiring through his generosity with advice, equipment, and support. I thank him and Marsha Nagler for their very important contributions.

I especially want to acknowledge David Charlsen for his brilliant design work and his telepathic sensitivity to my goals. I am lucky to have joined with David, as well as to have teamed with Simon & Schuster. I want to express my appreciation to all those at S & S who took this project to heart, particularly Jack McKeown, Caroline Herter, Patty Leasure, and Mary Kapp.

Gretchen Berggruen, Jennifer Weiss, and my dear Meredith Weiss have been great cheerleaders and friends. Thank you so much. I would also like to acknowledge Gordon Bermak for his role in helping define the tone and substance of the book. The gang at the Imperial House has always supplied humor and intellectual stimulation, especially Leo Jolson, Sherri Warner, Betty Berger, and Milton Wynn. Norman Kleeblatt at the Jewish Museum (New York City) and Margo Bloom at The National Museum of American Jewish History (Philadelphia) have been extremely supportive at times when I needed a jumpstart to get my battery charged. I also appreciate the creative freedom I was given by Mark McDonald and Martha Caig at Skylight & Sun, Incorporated.

Clearly, there is something magical about South Beach. Many fine photographers have been inspired there over the years. I have had the benefit of exchanging images and anecdotes with Gay Block, Gary Monroe, and David Scheinbaum, and the pleasure of seeing wonderful photographs by Andy Sweet, Mary Ellen Mark, and Jerome Liebling, among others. The source of this magnetic attraction has to be the people of South Beach, who not only let you into their lives, but into their souls. Some of the special souls I have encountered in South Beach are Sussie Feld, Minnie Zelman, Dorothy Olick, Max Goldseger, Rose Silverman, Jennie Hollander, Celia Flax, Jack Scop, Bessie Speyer, Ziggy Schwartz, Greta Kirschmann, Rabbi Jacob Katz, Dora Jacob, Jack Markowitz, Dorothy Simmons, Rabbi Sholom Blank, and Saul and Rachel Rabinowitz.

For those who would like more exposure to the brilliant mind of Isaac Bashevis Singer, I would recommend two books that helped me prepare for our talks: *Conversations with Isaac Bashevis Singer*, Isaac Bashevis Singer and Richard Burgin (Doubleday & Co., Inc., 1985) and *Isaac Bashevis Singer, The Magician of West 86th Street*, Paul Kersh (The Dial Press, 1979).